My Emotions

BORED

A Crabtree Roots Book

AMY CULLIFORD

CRABTREE
Publishing Company
www.crabtreebooks.com

School-to-Home Support for Caregivers and Teachers

This book helps children grow by letting them practice reading. Here are a few guiding questions to help the reader with building his or her comprehension skills. Possible answers appear here in red.

Before Reading:

• What do I think this book is about?
  - *This book is about feeling bored.*
  - *This book is about what feeling bored looks or feels like.*

• What do I want to learn about this topic?
  - *I want to learn what makes people feel bored.*
  - *I want to learn what feeling bored looks like.*

During Reading:

• I wonder why...
  - *I wonder why we yawn when we are bored.*
  - *I wonder what we can do when we are bored.*

• What have I learned so far?
  - *I have learned that you can read if you are bored.*
  - *I have learned that you can play a game if you are bored.*

After Reading:

• What details did I learn about this topic?
  - *I have learned that it is okay to feel bored.*
  - *I have learned that there are many things you can do when you feel bored.*

• Read the book again and look for the vocabulary words.
  - *I see the word **rains** on page 4 and the word **yawn** on page 6. The other vocabulary words are found on page 14.*

I am **bored**.

I am bored when
it **rains**.

I **yawn** when I am bored.

I am bored in the **car**.

I **read** when I am bored.

I play a **game** when I am bored.

When do you
feel bored?

Word List
Sight Words

a	I	the
am	it	when
do	play	you

Words to Know

bored

car

game

rains

read

yawn

40 Words

I am **bored**.

I am bored when it **rains**.

I **yawn** when I am bored.

I am bored in the **car**.

I **read** when I am bored.

I play a **game** when I am bored.

When do you feel bored?

CRABTREE
Publishing Company

Written by: Amy Culliford

Designed by: Rhea Wallace

Series Development: James Earley

Proofreader: Ellen Rodger

Educational Consultant: Marie Lemke M.Ed.

Photographs:

Shutterstock: Juan Pablo Gonzáález: cover; diplomedia:
   p. 1; Syda Productions: p. 3, 14; GOLFX: p. 5, 14;
   airdone: p. 7, 14; Leszek Glasner: p. 8-9, 14; Zurijeta:
   p. 10, 14; Motortion Films: p. 11, 14; fizkes: p. 13

My Emotions

BORED

Library and Archives Canada Cataloguing in Publication

Title: Bored / Amy Culliford.

Names: Culliford, Amy, 1992- author.

Description: Series statement: My emotions |
   "A Crabtree roots book".

Identifiers: Canadiana (print) 20210156678 |
   Canadiana (ebook) 20210156686 |
   ISBN 9781427139634 (hardcover) |
   ISBN 9781427139696 (softcover) |
   ISBN 9781427133403 (HTML) |
   ISBN 9781427139757 (read-along ebook) |
   ISBN 9781427134004 (EPUB)

Subjects: LCSH: Boredom—Juvenile literature.

Classification: LCC BF575.B67 C85 2021 |
   DDC j152.4—dc23

Library of Congress Cataloging-in-Publication Data

Names: Culliford, Amy, 1992- author.

Title: Bored / Amy Culliford.

Description: New York : Crabtree Publishing, 2021. | Series: My
   emotions, a crabtree roots book | Includes index.

Identifiers: LCCN 2021009518 (print) |
   LCCN 2021009519 (ebook) |
   ISBN 9781427139634 (hardcover) |
   ISBN 9781427139696 (paperback) |
   ISBN 9781427133403 (ebook) |
   ISBN 9781427134004 (epub) |
   ISBN 9781427139757 (read along)

Subjects: LCSH: Boredom--Juvenile literature. | Emotions in
   children--Juvenile literature.

Classification: LCC BF575.B67 C845 2021 (print) | LCC BF575.
   B67 (ebook) | DDC 152.4--dc23

LC record available at https://lccn.loc.gov/2021009518

LC ebook record available at https://lccn.loc.gov/2021009519

Crabtree Publishing Company

www.crabtreebooks.com   1-800-387-7650

Printed in the U.S.A./062021/CG20210401

Published in the United States
Crabtree Publishing
347 Fifth Avenue, Suite 1402-145
New York, NY, 10016

Published in Canada
Crabtree Publishing
616 Welland Ave.
St. Catharines, Ontario L2M 5V6